# BASICS OF RADIATION

M. PERIYASAMY | V. MANIVEL | N. KANNADASAN | S. CHRISTOBHER

# Contents


1. Sources Of Radiation     1

2. Types Of Radiation     5

3. Radiation Hazard Warning Signs     9

4. Glossary Of Radiological Terms     11

5. Bibliography     16

# CHAPTER ONE

# SOURCES OF RADIATION

The energy emitted from a source is generally referred to as radiation. In other words, radiation is the emission and propagation of waves transmitting energy through space or some medium (Example: Emission and propagation of electromagnetic, sound, or elastic waves). Radiation is energy given off by matter in the form of rays or high-speed particles. All the matter in the world is made up of atoms. In contrast, the atoms are composed of a nucleus containing minute particles (protons and neutrons), and the atom's outer shells contain other particles (electrons). The nucleus has a positive charge, while the electrons have a negative charge. These forces within the atom work toward a robust and stable balance by getting rid of excess atomic energy (**radioactivity**). The extra energy emitted from unstable nuclei produces the spontaneous emission called **radiation**.

Radioactivity is a part of our earth and is present throughout the environment. The sources of radiation are divided into two groups as shown below.

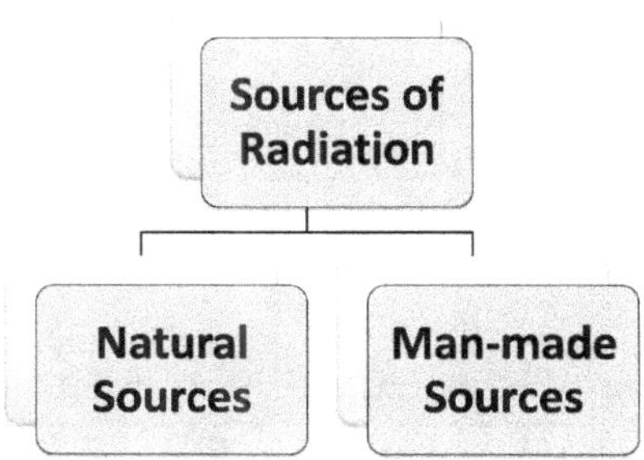


Fig. 1: Sources of Radiation

## *1.1. Natural Sources of Radiation*

Man has constantly been exposed to natural radiation arising from the earth and outside the planet. Inhalation and ingestion of radionuclides from air, food, and water is the primary source of natural radiation exposure to man. Another radioactive source is the naturally occurring materials present in its crust, the floors, and walls. Radon (a naturally-occurring gas) is the primary source of natural radiation which emanates from rocks and soil. Key source of natural radiation at high altitudes is cosmic rays (radiation received from outer space).

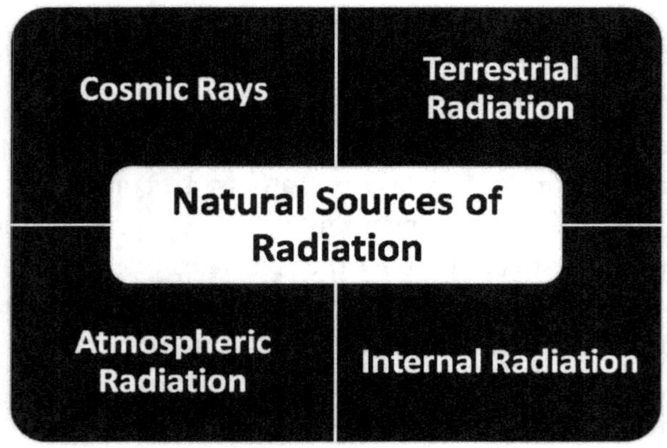


**Fig. 2: Natural Sources of Radiation**

Let's have a look on different natural sources of radiation.

- **Cosmic rays:** Cosmic rays are the photon particles received from the earth's atmosphere. They are also called space radiation. Owing to the shielding effect of the atmosphere, the intensity of cosmic rays increases with altitude above sea level.

- **Terrestrial radiation:** Terrestrial radiation emission originates from the radioactive materials present in the rocks, soils, and minerals. Radon (Rn) is the main terrestrial radiation and is produced through the decay of $^{226}$Ra (radium-226). Potassium ($^{40}$K), as well as the isotopes of thorium (Th) and uranium (U) is some other sources of terrestrial radiation.

- **Atmospheric radiation:** The external radiation dose from the radioactive gases in the atmosphere is rather small. The most common radioactive gases in the air are radon and thoron.

- **Internal radiation:** The presence of radioactive material in the environment results in internal exposure to the body. The human body itself contains isotopes of potassium (40K), rubidium (87Rb), and carbon (14C) in the blood and bones, which also contributes much to internal exposure.

## 1.2. Man Made Sources of Radiation

Human radiation exposure also comes from artificial sources. Artificial radiation sources are used for nuclear power generation and various industrial and research applications. The fallout from nuclear explosives testing, and small quantities of radioactive materials released to the environment from coal and nuclear power plants, are the primary sources of radiation exposure to man. Today, the most common human-made sources of radiation are medical devices used for diagnosis and treatments, including X-ray machines. Radiation also released from various consumer products.

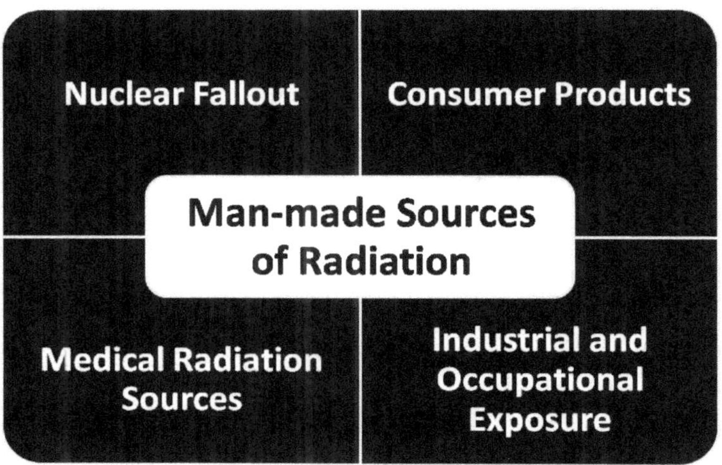


Fig. 3: Man-made Sources of Radiation

Brief account on various man-made sources of radiation is given below.

- **Nuclear fallout:** Nuclear explosions liberate a large amount of energy in the form of heat, light, ionizing radiation, and many radioactive substances. Cesium-137 and Strontium-90 are liberated in large amounts and remain radioactive for many years. Other radioactive substances such as Carbon-14 and Iodine-131 are also released during nuclear fallout.

- **Consumer products:** Consumer products such as wristwatches, clocks, luminous markers, televisions, and ionization smoke detectors contain radiations in mild quantity. Smoking tobacco products and building materials also act as the artificial sources of radiation.

- **Medical radiation sources:** Medical radiation sourcesare the major contributor to artificial radiation in man. Radiographic techniques, dental, and other medical X-rays are used for diagnostic purposes. A variety of radioactive materials are used for the treatments of several diseases. Medical instruments and heat-sensitive products (plastic heart valves) are sterilized with the help of radiation sources.

- **Industrial and occupational exposure:** Emissions from nuclear facilities (uranium mines, fuel processing plants, and nuclear power plants), mineral extraction facilities, and during the transportation of radioactive materials are industrial sources of artificial radiation. Occupational radiation exposure is common among researchers, radiologists, medical/ dental practitioners, industrial and aviation workers.

# CHAPTER TWO

# TYPES OF RADIATION

Radiation can be either **ionizing** or **non-ionizing**, depending on how it affects matter. The electromagnetic spectrum (Fig. 4) shows the characteristic features of the ionizing and non-ionizing radiation.

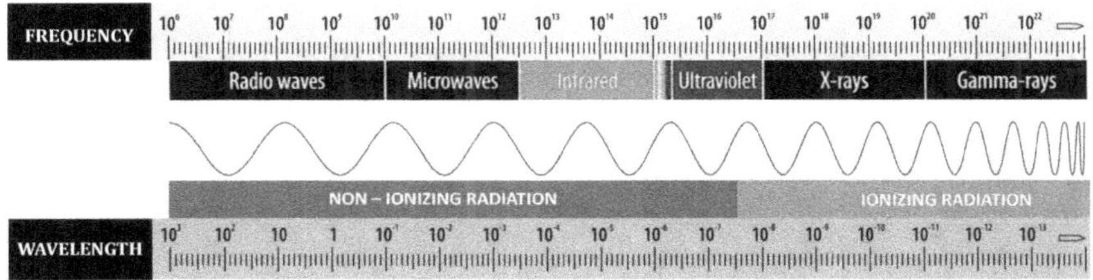

Fig. 4: Electromagnetic Spectrum

## 2.1. Non-ionizing radiation

Non-ionizing radiation refers to the low-frequency radiations in the electromagnetic wave spectrum like radio waves, microwaves, infrared, and visible light. This type of radiation deposits energy in the materials through which it passes, but it does not have sufficient energy to break molecular bonds or remove electrons from atoms (It can cause molecules to move in an atom but it cannot remove electrons). Hence non-ionizing is potentially less harmful than the ionizing radiation. The best-known proven effect of non-ionizing radiation is heating of tissues. Brief description about different types non-ionizing radiations are given as follows.

- **Radiowaves:** Radio waves are a type of electromagnetic radiation best-known for their use in communication technologies, such as television, mobile phones and radios. These devices receive radio waves and convert them to mechanical vibrations in the speaker to create sound waves.

- **Microwaves:** Microwaves heat an object on which they are incident. This property is used in electrical appliances such as a microwave oven that are used in drying materials and households for the preparation of food. Microwaves are widely used in modern technology such as point to point communication links and wireless networks.

- **Infrared:** Infrared radiation is used in industrial, scientific, military, commercial, and medical applications. Night-vision devices using active near-infrared illumination allow people or animals to be observed without the observer being detected. Infrared thermal-imaging cameras are used for different applications in various fields.

- **Visible light:** Visible light is the only part of the electromagnetic spectrum that human eyes can detect. The different wavelengths of visible light are seen as the colors of the rainbow: red, orange, yellow, green, blue, indigo, and violet.

- **Ultraviolet:** Ultraviolet is a form of electromagnetic radiation present in sunlight. It is also produced by electric arcs and specialized lights, such as mercury-vapor lamps, tanning lamps, and black lights. They are not considered as an ionizing radiation as the photons lack the energy to ionize atoms, it can cause chemical reactions and causes many substances to glow or fluoresce.

## 2.2. Ionizing Radiation

The term Ionizing radiation is applied to the energy released by atoms that travel in electromagnetic waves (gamma or X-rays) or particles (neutrons, beta, or alpha). Ionizing radiation is more energetic than non-ionizing radiation. When ionizing radiation passes through material, it deposits enough energy to break molecular bonds and displace (or remove) electrons from atoms. The spontaneous disintegration of atoms (radioactivity) results in the emission of excess energy (ionizing radiation). The unstable elements which disintegrate and emit ionizing radiation are called radionuclides. Ionizing radiation can change the chemical state of matter, which may cause changes in living cells of plants, animals and humans.

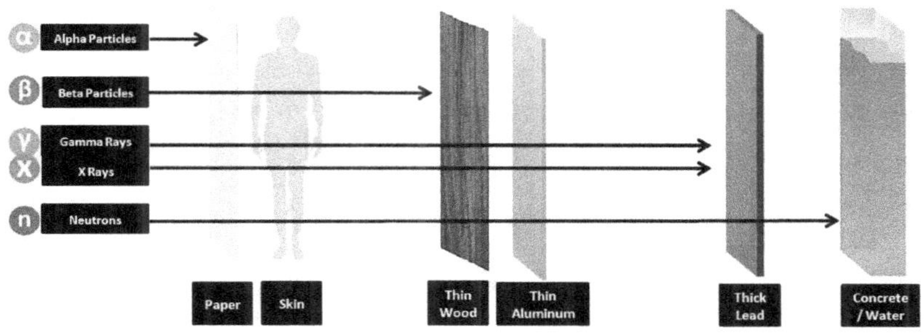


**Fig. 5: Penetration power of Ionizing radiation**

Ionizing radiation has divided into five different types as follows.

- **Alpha Particles**: Alpha particles denoted as 'α'. These are positively charged particles made up of protons and a couple of neutrons. They are emitted from naturally occurring materials or man-made elements. Alpha radiation has low penetration power (typically a few micrometers); hence it can be blocked by a sheet of paper, skin, or even a few inches of air. Internal exposure to alpha-emitting materials through inhalation ingestion or drinking may cause biological damage.

- **Beta Particles:** Beta particles denoted as ' β '. It consists of electrons, thus having a negative charge. Beta particles consist of high-energy, high-speed positrons or electrons released by radioactive nuclei. These fast-moving particles are lighter than alpha particles with high penetration power than alpha particles. Beta emitters have medical applications in the treatment of eye disease. They can be blocked by an aluminum sheet, glass, plastic, or a wood block with a few millimeters of thickness. It does not usually penetrate beyond the top layer of the skin. Inhalation/

ingestion of these materials is hazardous; even significant exposures causes skin burns.

- **Gamma Rays:** Gamma-ray is denoted as '$\gamma$.' Gamma is not a charged particle and does not have mass. They are electromagnetic radiation similar to visible light but have much higher energy. It has low ionization powers but has the shortest wavelength have high penetration power. Gamma rays emit along with alpha or beta particles during radioactive decay. Depending on their energy, Gamma rays can pass through the human body, and thick walls of concrete or lead can stop it. Gamma rays are hazardous for the entire body. It can easily penetrate barriers such as skin and clothing. It causes severe damage when absorbed by living cells and can damage tissues and DNA.

- **X-Rays:** X-rays are high-energy photons with a remarkable ability to penetrate other materials. It can travel great distances at the speed of light. X-rays can be produced naturally also with machines using electricity. X-rays have applications in medical (static imaging of body parts) and industrial (locating defects in welds) fields. X-rays can be blocked by using high thickness concrete or any dense materials such as lead.

  *"Note: Gamma rays are identical to x-rays except in their place of origin. X-rays are generated in collisions between electrons and atoms, whereas gamma rays are emitted spontaneously from the nuclei of unstable atoms."*

- **Neutrons:** Neutrons are high-speed nuclear particles with exceptional ability to penetrate other materials. Neutrons are uncharged; they do not produce ionization directly. These particles have the capability of neutron activation (converting an object into radioactive material). Ionization is caused by charged particles produced during collisions with atomic nuclei. It can travel great distances in air and require very thick hydrogen-containing materials (such as concrete or water) to block them. Neutron radiation primarily occurs inside a nuclear reactor, where many feet of water provide adequate shielding.

# CHAPTER THREE

# RADIATION HAZARD WARNING SIGNS

Hazard symbols or warning symbols are recognisable symbols designed to warn about hazardous or dangerous materials, locations, or objects. Let's have a look on diffeent standard radiation hazard warning sings used.

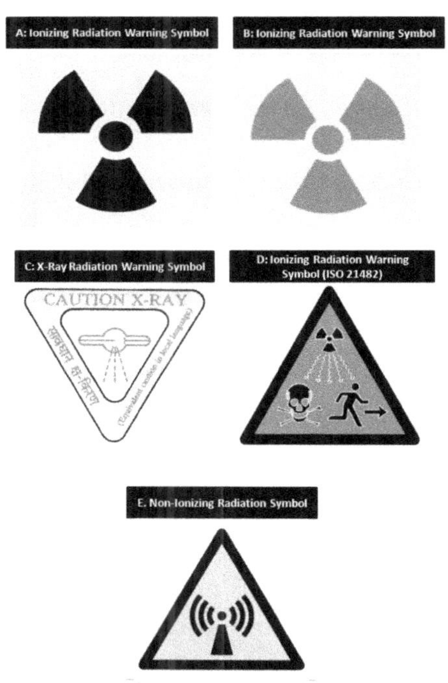

Fig. 6: Radiation hazard warning signs

## 3.1. Ionizing-Radiation Warning Symbol

The international radiation symbol is a trefoil around a small central circle representing radiation from an atom. Trefoil ionizing radiation symbols with magenta or black propellers on yellow background are generally used (**Fig. 6A-B**). The sign is commonly referred to as a radioactivity warning sign, but it is actually a warning sign of ionizing radiation. Ionizing radiation is a much broader category than radioactivity alone, as many non-radioactive sources also emit potentially dangerous levels of ionizing radiation.

## 3.2. X-Ray Radiation Warrning Symbol

The inverted triangle symbol (**Fig. 6C**) is particularly used for radiation hazard associated with an X-ray machine. According to the Atomic Energy Regulatory Board (AERB) guidelines in india, it is the mandatory symbol that has to be posted in and around a facility using an X-ray machine.

## 3.3. Ionizing Radiation Warning Symbol (ISO 21482)

The red ionizing radiation warning symbol (ISO 21482) was launched in 2007. The new symbol (**Fig. 6D**) is a universal radiation warning to supplement the existing trefoil symbol. It is intended to caution about the dangerous sources capable of causing death or serious injury. It should be placed on the device housing the source, as a warning not to dismantle the device or to get any closer. The new symbol is aimed at alerting anyone, anywhere to the potential dangers of being close to a large source of ionizing radiation.

## 3.4. Non-Ionizing Radiation Warning Symbol

Non-ionizing radiation can also reach potentially dangerous levels, but this warning sign is different from the trefoil ionizing radiation warning symbol. The symbol (**Fig. 6D**) consist of a circle with three arc-shaped lines of increasing length on each side symmetrically located, with a trapezoid underneath. It is generally used to warn of workplace dangers from non-ionizing radiation.

# CHAPTER FOUR

# GLOSSARY OF RADIOLOGICAL TERMS

- **Absorbed dose:** The energy imparted by ionizing radiation to a suitably small volume of matter divided by the mass of that volume. Unit gray, symbol Gy. 1 Gy = 1 joule per kilogram.

- **Actinides:** A group of 15 *elements* with *atomic number* from that of actinium (89) to lawrencium (103) inclusive. All are *radioactive*. Group includes uranium, plutonium, americium, and curium.

- **Activity:** The rate at which nuclear transformations occur in a *radioactive material*. Used as a measure of the amount of a *radionuclide* present. Unit becquerel, symbol Bq. 1 Bq = 1 transformation per second.

- **Alpha particle:** A particle consisting of two *protons* plus two *neutrons* (i.e. the *nucleus* of a helium *atom*) emitted by a *radionuclide*.

- **Becquerel:** The becquerel (Bq) is the SI derived unit of radioactivity. One becquerel is defined as the activity of a quantity of radioactive material in which one nucleus decays per second.

- **Beta particle:** An *electron* or *positron* which has been emitted by an atomic *nucleus* or *neutron* in a nuclear transformation.

- **Brachytherapy:** The use of sealed radioactive sources in or on the body for treating certain types of cancer.

- **Collective dose:** An expression for the aggregate radiation dose incurred by a population defined as the product of the number of individuals exposed to a source and their average radiation dose.

- **Collective effective dose:** The quantity obtained by adding the *effective doses* received by all of the people in a defined population (often all of the people exposed to *radiation* from a particular source). Unit man sievert, symbol man Sv. Frequently abbreviated to collective dose.

- **Cosmic rays:** High energy *ionizing radiation* from outer space. Have a complex composition at the surface of the Earth.

- **Decay product:** A *nuclide* or *radionuclide* produced by *decay*. It may be formed directly from decay of a *radionuclide* or as a result of a series of *decays* through several *radionuclides*. Sometimes referred to as progeny or daughters.

- **Decay:** The process of spontaneous transformation of a *radionuclide* or the decrease in the activity of a *radioactive* substance as a result of this process.

- **Diagnostic radiology:** The use of radiation (e.g. *X rays*) or radioactive materials in medicine for identifying disease or injury in patients.

- **Dose:** General term for a measure of the energy deposited by *radiation* in a target. See the more specific terms *absorbed dose, equivalent dose, effective dose* and *collective effective dose*. Frequently used for *effective dose*.

- **Effective dose:** A measure of *dose* designed to reflect the amount of *radiation detriment* likely to result from the *dose*. Obtained by multiplying the *equivalent dose* to each tissue or organ by an appropriate tissue weighting factor and summing the products. Unit sievert, symbol Sv.

- **Equivalent dose:** A measure of the *dose* to a tissue or organ designed to reflect the amount of harm caused to the tissue or organ. Obtained by multiplying the *absorbed dose* by a radiation weighting factor to allow for the different effectiveness of the various types of *radiation* in causing harm to tissue. Unit sievert, symbol Sv.

- **Erythema:** Reddening of the skin caused by dilation of blood vessels. Can occur as a result of high *radiation doses.*

- **Excitation:** A process by which *radiation* imparts energy to an *atom* or *molecule* without causing *ionization.* The energy may be absorbed by the *nucleus* or the *electrons,* and may be released in the form of *radiation* when the *atom* or *molecule* 'relaxes'.

- **Fallout:** Airborne radioactive material from the testing of nuclear weapons or nuclear accidents deposited on the Earth's surface.

- **Gamma ray:** Penetrating electromagnetic radiation emitted by an atomic nucleus during radioactive decay and having wavelengths much shorter than those of visible light.

- **Geiger–Müller tube:** A glass or metal envelope containing a gas at low pressure and two electrodes. *Ionizing radiation* causes discharges, which are registered as electric pulses in a counter. The number of pulses is related to *dose.*

- **Gray:** The gray is a derived unit of ionizing radiation dose in the International System of Units. It is defined as the absorption of one joule of radiation energy per kilogram of matter.

- **Half-life:** For a *radionuclide,* the time required for the *activity* to decrease, by a radioactive decay process, by half. Symbol $t1/2.$

- **Ionization:** The process by which an *atom* or *molecule* acquires or loses an electric charge. The production of *ions.*

- **Ionizing radiation:** For the purposes of *radiation protection, radiation* capable of producing ion pairs in biological material(s). Examples are *alpha particles, gamma rays, X rays* and *neutrons.*

- **Irradiation:** The act of being exposed to radiation. It can be intentional, for example through industrial irradiation to sterilize medical equipment, or accidental, for example through proximity to a source that emits radiation. Irradiation does not usually result in radioactive contamination, but damage can occur depending on the dose received.

- **Isotopes:** *Nuclides* with the same number of *protons* but different numbers of *neutrons*. Not a synonym for nuclide.

- **Non-ionizing radiation:** *Radiation* that is not *ionizing radiation*. Examples are *ultraviolet radiation, visible light, infrared radiation* and *radiofrequency radiation*.

- **Nuclear medicine:** The use of *radionuclides* for diagnosing or treating disease in patients.

- **Nuclide:** A species of *atom* characterized by the number of *protons* and *neutrons* and the energy state of the *nucleus*.

- **Photon:** A quantum of *electromagnetic radiation*.

- **Radiation detriment:** The total harm that would eventually be experienced by an exposed person or group and their descendants as a result of their *exposure* to *radiation*.

- **Radiation:** Energy, in the form of waves or particles, propagating through space. Frequently used for *ionizing radiation* in the text, except when it is necessary to avoid confusion with *non-ionizing radiation*.

- **Radioactive:** Exhibiting *radioactivity*. For legal and regulatory purposes, the meaning of *radioactive* is often restricted to those materials designated in national law or by a *regulatory body* as being subject to regulatory control because of their *radioactivity*.

- **Radioactivity:** The phenomenon whereby atoms undergo spontaneous random disintegration, usually accompanied by the emission of *radiation*.

- **Radiobiology:** The study of the effects of *ionizing radiation* on living things.

- **Radionuclide:** A *radioactive nuclide.*

- **Radiotherapy:** The use of radiation beams for treating disease, usually cancer, in patients.

- **Scintillation counter:** A device containing material that emits light flashes when exposed to *ionizing radiation.* The flashes are converted to electric pulses which are counted. The number of pulses is related to *dose.*

- **Sievert:** The sievert is a derived unit of ionizing radiation dose in the International System of Units and is a measure of the health effect of low levels of ionizing radiation on the human body.

- **Thermoluminescent material:** Material which, when heated, releases visible light in proportion to the amount of *radiation* to which it has been exposed.

# CHAPTER FIVE

# BIBLIOGRAPHY


- Atwood, D.A., 2010. Radionuclide in the environment. UK: Jhon Willy & Sons Ltd

- Choppin, G., Liljenzin, J.O. and Rydberg, J., 2002. Radiochemistry and nuclear chemistry. Butterworth-Heinemann.

- Friedlander, G., Kennedy, J.W., Macias, E.S. and Miller, J.M., 1981. Nuclear and radiochemistry. John Wiley & Sons.

- IAEA. 2004. Radiation, People and the Environment. Vienna, International Atomic Energy Agency.

- ICRP, 2015. Radiological Protection in Cone Beam Computed Tomography (CBCT). ICRP Publication 129. Ann. ICRP 44(1).

- International Commission on Non-Ionizing Radiation Protection, 2020. Principles for non-ionizing radiation protection. Health physics, 118(5), pp.477-482.

- Kratz, J.V., 2022. Nuclear and radiochemistry: Fundamentals and applications. John Wiley & Sons.

- Lieser, K.H., 2008. Nuclear and radiochemistry: fundamentals and applications. John Wiley & Sons.

- Park, K., 2005. Textbook of Preventive and Social Medicine (18th Edition). Bhanot Publisher. Jabalpur, India.

- Saha G.B., 2001. Physics and Radiobiology of Nuclear Medicine. Springer, New York.

- UNSCEAR. 2000. Sources and effects of ionizing radiation. United Nations Scientific Committee on the Effects of Atomic Radiation. Report to the General Assembly, United Nations, New York, USA.